The Johnstone Twins

An Appreciation of
Janet Johnstone (1928-1979) & Anne Grahame Johnstone (1928-1998)

PHILIP KELLEWAY

Title page photograph: *Janet Johnstone (standing) and*
Anne Grahame Johnstone (sitting) in their London studio.

First published in Great Britain in 2013

British Library Cataloguing-in-Publication Data
A CIP record for this title is available from the British
Library

ISBN 978 1 906690 49 6

HALSTAR
Halsgrove House,
Ryelands Business Park, Bagley Road,
Wellington, Somerset TA21 9PZ
Tel: 01823 653777   Fax: 01823 216796
email: sales@halsgrove.com

Part of the Halsgrove group of companies
Information on all Halsgrove titles is
available at: www.halsgrove.com

Printed in China by Everbest Printing Co Ltd

Contents

foreword

by Captain E. M. G. Johnstone RN (Retd.)

My memories of Janet and Anne are enduring. We always had such fun together, riding our ponies and painting in the nursery. They were the kindest sisters a brother could have. I was allowed into their world, and we formed a fun-loving trio.

They were dedicated artists working every day of their lives, listening to music, and creating beauty. Our mother, Doris Zinkeisen, was one of Britain's most eminent women artists of her day. My sisters followed in her footsteps. My children have similarly gone on to lead creative lives. My son, Andrew, is a photographer and film maker. Of my daughters, Jemima, is an interior decorator, and Charlotte is a portrait painter.

Philip Kelleway's monograph is a sensitive and perceptive view of my sisters' lives and work. I hope you will enjoy reading Philip Kelleway's essay and looking at the numerous reproductions of my sisters' paintings and drawings as much as I have.

Acknowledgements

During the course of compiling this book on the Johnstone twins I have received help and advice from many individuals. I have been working on the Zinkeisen sisters and their daughters on and off for over a decade. My greatest debt of gratitude for continued support with my art-historical research endeavours in connection with the Zinkeisen clan is to the related families themselves. Murray Johnstone, Doris Zinkeisen's son and the brother of the Johnstone twins, together with his wife Elisabeth, have remained staunchly supportive of this project. The photographer and film-maker Andrew Johnstone, Murray's son, was particularly helpful with background information on the twins and with the supply of images. For further pictures of some paintings and drawings in private hands, I am grateful to the artist Tristan Sam Weller, who provided me with numerous images, a task he carried out with great skill and care at a time he was snowed under with other work. Tristan Sam Weller's mother, the artist Julia Heseltine, who is the daughter of Anna Zinkeisen and a first cousin to the Johnstone twins, was similarly forthcoming with information and was proactive in putting me in touch with people.

I also acknowledge gratefully the following, who assisted me, sometimes more than they may realise: Debbie Barnes (Assistant Curator of Human History, Christchurch Mansion, Ipswich, Suffolk); Geoff and Cynthia Hassell; Hannah Izod (Archivist, Seven Stories, National Centre for Children's Books, Newcastle upon Tyne); Mary May; Julian Royle; Sean Noel (Associate Director, Howard Gotlieb Archival Research Center, Boston University); the late Josephine Walpole; Elly White and all her colleagues (The Great British Card Company, Gloucester); Chris Wilcox (Commercial Director, The Great British Card Company, Gloucester).

I must thank Professor Ludmilla Jordanova for opening my eyes, and my parents, John and Eugenie Kelleway, for introducing me to Doris Zinkeisen and Anne Grahame Johnstone in the first place many years ago. Finally, I would particularly like to thank my wife, Elisabeth, and our daughters, Eve Florence and Hannah Odessa, who continue to accommodate my need to study Art History. None of the above mentioned are responsible for any errors, or distortions, which may inadvertently remain in the book, as these are entirely my own.

Illustration Acknowledgements: Many of the illustrations were provided by The Great British Card Company from their archives in Gloucester, or photographed by Tristan Sam Weller from the collection of Murray Johnstone, brother of the Johnstone twins. Christchurch Mansion in Ipswich and the Howard Gotlieb Archival Research Center at Boston University in the United States of America provided copies of pictures by the Johnstone twins from their collections, for which the author is truly grateful. Additional images were supplied by the owners of the pictures, including Andrew Johnstone. The author and publisher are also grateful to the National Portrait Gallery in London for permission to use Doris Zinkeisen's 1929 self-portrait from their archives. Every effort has been made to contact the holders of the illustrative material contained in this book. Any omissions are inadvertent and will receive appropriate redress and be corrected in future editions, provided the publisher and author are notified in writing. Dimensions have not been included as these are often unknown.

A scene with children and their umbrellas in the rain by Janet Johnstone & Anne Grahame Johnstone.

The Pony Who Came to Tea

Now and then Victoria, the dun-coloured pony and one of the numerous pets belonging to the children's book illustrators Janet Johnstone (1928-1979) and Anne Grahame Johnstone (1928-1998), was invited to tea. In the mid-1970s a reporter was sent from the popular magazine *Woman's Weekly* to interview the twins at their home, The White House, situated in rural Suffolk between Badingham and Framlingham in England. Imagine the reporter's genuine astonishment when Victoria wandered into the well-appointed dining room via a side door to the garden, although this was precisely the sort of harmlessly eccentric incident, which could occur from time to time at The White House when the Johnstone twins lived there.

A letter to some friends of the twins named Betty and Anthony Reid dated 2nd January 1973 and now held at Sevenstories (The Centre for Children's Books) in Newcastle upon Tyne [Ref. No. JAJ 08/01/06] describes the pony, Victoria, coming into the dining room on Christmas Day: "she [Victoria] all but walked in, crackers, lights, candles, people shouting & all!" For the twins, their wider family, and their circle of friends, having a pony in the dining room was unusual, but perfectly

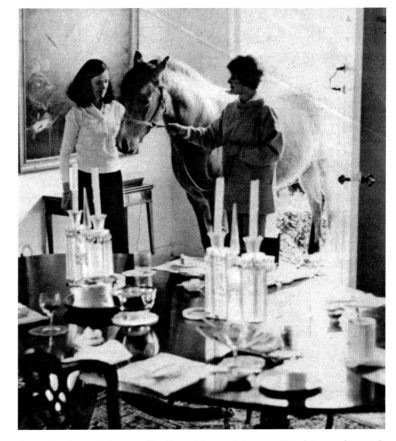

Anne Grahame Johnstone (Left) and Janet Johnstone (Right) together with their pony Victoria in the dining room of The White House in Badingham, Suffolk.

congenial behaviour. This then is a colourful glimpse into the unconventional lives led by the Johnstone twins. Here at the Suffolk home of the twins, the fanciful could harmoniously coexist in their imagination and reality. It is this sentiment, or way of perception, that the twins often capture in their illustrations.

In my opinion the Johnstone twins have not received the critical attention they deserve. This is true, however, of children's book illustration in general. For most grown-ups childhood is but a fleeting period of life. All that goes with it, including illustrated children's books, are normally left behind and forgotten – genuine enthusiasts for the genre and primary teachers excepted. Parenthood and grandparenthood may for a short time rekindle interest in children's books, but unavoidably always as an outsider, and never with the excitement of a child's first impression. It is perhaps not unexpected, therefore, that write-ups about children's books are thin on the ground, in spite of all the persistent brouhaha arising from political discussions of early-years education and the experience of childhood in modern day society. This book is intended to celebrate the life and artistic output of the Johnstone twins. It will probably appeal most to those readers already familiar with some of their oeuvre, but may find favour amongst a new audience.

The Johnstone twins left a prodigious volume of work. They illustrated in excess of one hundred books in addition to designs for cards, calendars, labels, wrapping paper, tins, and jigsaws. Early in their careers the twins were also involved in pioneering children's television broadcasts, as will be discussed further later, including *Andy Pandy* and *Bill and Ben the Flower Pot Men*, in particular illustrating the spin-off published annuals and weekly children's comic strips. Because the Johnstone twins were so prolific some sort of elimination process has to be deployed in order to avoid unnecessary repetition. My choice is governed by personal preference and the availability of sources. Notwithstanding this I think the book includes a good cross section of the artistic work of the Johnstone twins. This monograph on the Johnstone twins also provides a window into the preoccupations of their often enchantingly whimsical imaginations, which were just occasionally indistinguishable from their everyday lives. The Johnstone twins did, after all, keep in touch with their inner child and inhabited a sphere where ponies could be friends and actually come to tea.

Early Life

Janet Johnstone and Anne Grahame Johnstone were born on the 1st June, 1928 in London. Janet was the older twin being born just 20 minutes before Anne. Almost two years later the twins were joined by a brother, Murray, who was born on the 24th March, 1930. Their father, Captain Grahame Johnstone D.S.C., R.N.V.R. (d.1946), was a director at Johnny Walker Whisky, a captain in the Royal Naval Volunteer Reserve, and stepson of the eminent businessman Baron James Stevenson. Their mother was the Scottish-born artist and designer Doris Clare Zinkeisen (1897-1991). In her inter-war heyday Doris Zinkeisen was as famous in the press for her fabulous looks and glamorous sense of dress, as she was for her sensational portraits and costume designs for the theatre and newly burgeoning film sector.

The Johnstones initially lived with their young family at 6 Chester Terrace close to Regent's Park in London. Their life can broadly be described as affluent, sophisticated, and chic. The young married Johnstones were firmly a part of the upper echelons of London society. The Johnstone twins' mother was

Murray Johnstone (Left), Janet Johnstone (Right) and Anne Grahame Johnstone (Centre) at Matts House, Thornby, Northamptonshire.

Doris Zinkeisen, "Self-portrait", 1929, oil on canvas. © National Portrait Gallery, London/The Estate of Doris Zinkeisen {6487}.

Doris Zinkeisen was the Johnstone twins' mother and one of the most glamorous and famous women artists of her generation.

Opposite page:
Top left: *Janet Johnstone (Left) and Anne Grahame Johnstone (Right).*

Bottom left: *Janet Johnstone (Left) and Anne Grahame Johnstone (Right) in the garden in London.*

Far right: *Janet Johnstone (Right) and Anne Grahame Johnstone (Left).*

Murray Johnstone (Right), Janet Johnstone (Centre) and Anne Grahame Johnstone (Left) at an exhibition of their mother's paintings.

never a conventional homemaker and continued to work as a painter and designer throughout her life. Doris Zinkeisen's work brought her into contact with some of the great personalities of the inter-war period and reads like a Who's Who of the distinguished and influential theatre and film people of their age, including the popular heart-throb Jack Buchanan, impresario Charles Cochran, theatrical all-rounder Noël Coward, the dancers and actresses Elsa Lanchester and Anna Neagle, as well as the film director Herbert Wilcox, to name but a few. Doris Zinkeisen remained a close friend of the great actor, producer and director Laurence Olivier after she worked on designs for a production of *Richard III* in 1944. It is also noteworthy that before her marriage to Grahame Johnstone, Doris Zinkeisen had been engaged to James Whale, who in the 1930s became the hugely influential Hollywood film director behind cult classics including *Frankenstein* (1931), *The Invisible Man* (1933), *The Bride of Frankenstein* (1935), and *Show Boat* (1936). Although they never married they remained life-long friends. So in addition to wealth and high social status, the Johnstone twins were brought up in an environment of great flair, creativity, and glamour as well.

During the Second World War the German air raids on London turned the Johnstone twins, along with countless others, into evacuees. Indeed, the family home at 6 Chester Terrace was struck by an incendiary device during the Blitz in 1940. For the duration of the war the Johnstone family moved to Matts House, a 'hunting lodge' rented from heirs to the Wills cigarette dynasty situated in Thornby, Northamptonshire. Here in Thornby the Johnstone children were joined by their younger cousin Julia Heseltine, who today is herself a celebrated portraitist and landscape artist, and the daughter of Doris's sister, Anna Zinkeisen, another hugely prominent painter and designer. The closeness of these two branches of the same family, both with strong artistic interests, is a significant aspect to the twins' upbringing and their creative background. The Zinkeisen sisters were also strong female role models for the Johnstone twins and their cousin Julia.

The country life experienced by the Johnstone twins during World War II was replaced once more by life in London, or boarding school at Heathfield, Ascot. Grahame Johnstone had just started working for Imperial Tobacco upon release from

A prize-winning painting by Anne Grahame Johnstone from her school days at Heathfield.

active duty in the armed services after the war had ended when he fell ill on a business trip to North Africa in 1946, which was to kill him. Having survived military action in two world wars his death was like a bolt from the blue. His sudden and unexpected death was sad and he was sorely missed. Grahame Johnstone's demise also imposed new and sudden financial constraints on his family. The newly purchased lease on a home in Hanover Terrace was deemed too expensive and quickly sold. Instead from 1946 to 1966 the twins lived with their mother in a comparatively modest yet still extremely spacious and smart apartment at 50 Albert Court in Kensington close to the Royal Albert Hall and Kensington Gardens. This period in the life of the twins at Albert Court also included several years training at art school.

An Arthur Rackhamesque fantasy by the Johnstone twins in the making.

16

Artistic Training

After leaving Heathfield, which Anne is known to have referred to as her "beastly boarding school", the twins trained at St Martin's School of Art. They began their studies just after the war had ended and when they were still teenagers. At that time St Martin's was jam packed with war veterans released from service in the armed forces, who had received grants to enable them to obtain some training of use down civvy street. Britain was at that point still under a system of rationing and everything was in short supply. Anne remarked once how nothing could be left lying around. Items of clothing and even canvases were prone to be pinched. One of the teachers who certainly taught the twins, whilst at St Martin's School of Art was the artist Clifford Webb. In addition to teaching Webb wrote and illustrated numerous children's books and is today perhaps best known for his illustrations for the first two books for children from the *Swallows and Amazons* sequence of novels by Arthur Ransome. Clifford Webb and his work were an important influence on the Johnstone twins, but there was further inspiration closer to home.

Although Doris Zinkeisen and her sister might not have encouraged, or influenced their daughters into considering art as a career path, the highly creative environment they inhabited must have acted as an important catalyst. In the 1930s one of Doris' most important commissions was to produce large-scale decorative murals for RMS *Queen Mary*. Amongst her work for the giant ship were two murals 11 feet by 9 feet. These murals were damaged during the Second World War when the liner was used as a troopship. After the war Doris was invited to rework these murals, which she carried out largely at her studio at Albert Court on hinged stretchers. The twins assisted their mother by filling in the backgrounds of the compositions. It is precisely this type of insight into the working life of a successful and influential artist, which would have been the Johnstone twins' prime source of influence. The inspiration of the Zinkeisen sisters can clearly be detected in the work of the twins, although their work remains steadfastly individualistic and distinctly their own at the same time. This is, however, a point I will return to later.

Other artists' work, beyond family members, which inspired the Johnstone twins includes the fantastic and sometimes grotesque illustrations by Edmund Dulac, the idyllic and delightful costume fantasies of Kate Greenaway, and the imaginative illustrations of Arthur Rackham. Further inspiration for the twins' art came from their shared passion for horses and love of literature, history, and the countryside.

Doris Zinkeisen, "The Artist's Daughters at The White House in Badingham, Suffolk, with their Pets", circa 1970, oil on canvas.
Picture by courtesy of Mallams Fine Art Auctioneers/Howell Lambert.

The Life of Ponies

As schoolgirls Janet and Anne wrote an unpublished book and illustrated it entitled *The Life of Ponies*. This prefigures their later career choices and enthusiasms, as illustrated in much of their work. In their early, formative lives as evacuees in the Northamptonshire countryside, the twins learnt to ride ponies. The whole family were horse enthusiasts, including their aunt Anna and her husband. The twins' parents were eager riders too. Indeed, Doris won numerous prizes for her horsemanship at important equestrian events, such as at the International Horse Show at Olympia where she won the Champion Lady Hack three years running from 1932 to 1934. The twins also grew fond of driving a pony and trap. When the twins moved with their mother to Suffolk they were pleased to finally be able to keep horses with them at home, rather than at livery, as had been the case whilst living in London.

In 1966 Doris Zinkeisen decided to move from London and her daughters joined her. Together they found The White House in Badingham, close to Framlingham in Suffolk. This house was not far from Doris's sister, Anna Zinkeisen, and niece, Julia Heseltine, who already lived most of the time at a delightful thatched cottage in Burgh, close to Woodbridge in Suffolk, when not

The White House in Badingham, Suffolk when the Johnstone twins lived there.

staying at their respective London homes. Already having family close by must have influenced the decision to move to Suffolk, where they could form a familial art colony. The White House was sold after Anne's death on the 25th May 1998 and her subsequent burial together with her twin in the same grave at St John Baptist church in Badingham. These years in Suffolk were to prove artistically productive and enjoyable. A group portrait by Doris from the early 1970s shows her daughters in the grounds of The White House, which forms the backdrop for the scene.

Interior scene of The White House in Badingham, Suffolk. Over the living room mantelpiece is a posthumous portrait of Janet Johnstone by Doris Zinkeisen.

Interior scene of The White House in Badingham, Suffolk. On the wall of the front entrance hall hangs Doris Zinkeisen's 1929 self-portrait.

Janet stands beside the dun mare Victoria and the Irish Wolfhound Fionn. Anne is seated beneath a large tree with Bruno the brown Burmese on her lap and is coaxing Ming the white Siamese towards her, whilst Comus the cavalier dog plays at her feet. The scene Doris painted may appear to some as unrealistically Arcadian in sentiment, but in this painting she did in fact capture accurately the idyllic way of country life she and her daughters led. In retrospect the group portrait is tinged with a considerable poignancy. It arouses a sense of sadness by virtue of the fact that on the 20th January 1979, just a few years after the portrait's creation, Janet perished of asphyxiation having been overcome by the fumes of a fire in the kitchen at The White House.

The ponies kept by Janet and Anne at The White House, as well as their other pets and menagerie of adopted animals, were frequently enlisted as models for their paintings. Time and again their pets inspire the twins and appear in their artwork, amongst them the three brown hens Henrietta, Marmalade, and Cottontail, the two black hens Dolly and Tortoiseshell, and their adopted tame pheasant, Daddydoodle. Drawings and paintings of ponies and horses abound the work of the twins. Anne also became skilled at painting crests and monograms on horse-drawn driving vehicles. The twins could often be spotted shopping in Framlingham, or on the country lanes around their Suffolk home, driving the pony Victoria to a restored two-wheeled trap decorated by Anne with the Johnstone Clan badge of a winged spur surrounded by a belt and motto. Heraldic carriage painting, however, always remained a sideline to Anne's (and her sister's) main career as an illustrator.

Subject Matter

The Johnstone twins produced illustrations for over one hundred books. With a few exceptions, most notably including the equestrian volume *Encyclopaedia of Driving* (1974) by the twins' friend Sallie Walrond, their illustrations were for children's books. I would suggest that an important aspect to understanding the creative work for children by the twins is their ability to see the world through children's eyes. As the twins remained childless spinsters living at home with their mother, it could be argued, albeit simplistically, that they were suspended in a state of arrested childhood. There is, however, a gulf between the inspiration of the childlike and the childish. I think also, that often the children painted by the twins are almost like their very own substitute offspring and represent the children they never had. The twins may have been mildly eccentric, but they had to live in the 'real' world of responsibilities, commitments, and chores too. Moreover, although much of the twins' artistic output appears to be unrealistic and escapist, their work is simultaneously rooted in real life.

The horses, ponies, and wild creatures great and small, the buildings and landscapes were often inspired by actual animals and places, though frequently adjusted for the purposes of the story. Indeed, the illustrations were always blended to suit the fantasies they carefully referred to and adorned. For example, the twins set about sketching Dandy, Folly, and Buzz, the Dalmatians of the authoress Dodie Smith, as the basis of the illustrations for *The Hundred and One Dalmatians* (1956). Also some of the scenes illustrated in this classic canine fantasy children's story were loosely based on places seen by the Johnstone twins on their trips around Essex when visiting Dodie Smith, with whom the twins remained lifelong friends, at her home in Finchingfield. It is also worth noting as a good example of the twins making use of things seen in the world around them, that the illustrations by the twins for Dodie Smith's *The Starlight Barking* (1967) include endpapers with recognisable scenes, amongst them Framlingham castle, as well as containing within the book a representation of the Thomas Gainsborough monument in Sudbury.

The Johnstone twins could make their illustrations forthrightly figurative, but they could also be whimsical, pleasantly dreamy, or sometimes a little frightening in order to capture the magical essence of particular fairy stories they had been commissioned to conjure up illustrations for. Their pictures are included in the books to act as aids to the story, to helpfully make clear key points in the text, to assist the reader in visualising what they regarded as exciting features within the narrative, but occasionally also to educate, and certainly always to entertain.

Doris Zinkeisen was famous for her work as a costume and set designer for the entertainments business. Her costumes for historical dramas were always accurate, although she often deliberately exaggerated the lines of the outfits, the aim being to add both period feel to the costume and some of her own distinctive flamboyant charm. The costumes depicted in the work of the twins carry on in a similar vein. The period costumes in the twins' illustrations are mined from actual historical modes of dress. Their period costumes should be seen as caricatured representations of sartorial styles of dress, which attractively 'romanticise' the past in a delightfully fanciful way without being overly sentimental. What must not be overlooked is the Johnstone twins' magnificent draftsmanship and elegance of composition.

Technique

The Johnstone twins always strove hard to link their illustrations to the written word. The finished results were seldom predictable. Each commission was taken extremely seriously by the twins and as professional artists they understood how to work under the dual pressures of time and cost constraints. To this end they both remained disciplined about their working hours. If disturbed whilst working in their studio the twins would playfully chorus, "Don't interrupt us, we are in the middle of a 'wash'", referring to a thin coating of paint, rather than the act of bathing.

The twins spent most days working whilst the daylight lasted, having breaks to tend to everyday chores and look after their numerous pets. Their studio housed a vast reference library, which they consulted time and again to ensure the accuracy of the scenes and costumes they painted and drew. It is precisely their meticulous attention to detail, which contributes to the appeal of their work. Prior to Janet's tragic early death the twins worked in tandem. They always worked in a shared studio passing drawings and paintings back and forth between them until they felt the work was finished. There were often four or more stages to many of their paintings. First they created a

drawing, which was traced. Their tracings in designers' layout pads were then used to make outlines for the second drawings for painting on, so keeping an unblemished, unpainted initial drawing for further reference later on, or in case of corrections. Their studio was sometimes referred to as the deep litter room as the floor could be covered in discarded sketches and paintings, which their brother referred to as their artistic 'jetsam'. The twins invariably worked while listening to music. A certain amount of specialisation did take place. Anne tended

Anne Grahame Johnstone. A sketch on layout pad paper for a painting representing children playing a game of tug of war.

Anne Grahame Johnstone. A sketch on layout pad paper for a painting of Oranges and Lemons.

to work on the costumes, whilst Janet focused on the animals. After Janet's death Anne received some initial assistance with drawing and painting horses from her mother and Anne became so adept at this that she was honoured to be elected a member of the Society of Equestrian Artists. Even when not in their studio engaged in remunerative drawing and painting, the twins would make line drawings on scraps of paper, as quasi-notes of reference for possible future use in compositions. They also had to take into account the demands of the publishers.

The twins usually worked in gouache, a type of opaque watercolour paint thickened and mingled with a preparation of gum, applied by brush to paper. They had to carefully choose colours which would reproduce well in the completed printed book. Publishers were quick to return paintings they did not quite like with annotations scribbled over them informing the twins what needed to be changed. On one occasion an employee at a publishing company had counted the number of whiskers on the representation of a cat and returned the paintings requesting that the feline character in question had to have the exact same number of whiskers in each and every instance. It would appear to be the case that illustrators are from time to time permitted artistic licence only with clipped wings. This in no way suggests that the twins subordinated their individual artistic expression to the publisher's demands, though always remained mindful of their needs.

Amongst a cache of letters held by the twins' brother are several relating to a commission to produce illustrations for the writer

Janet Johnstone & Anne Grahame Johnstone. This painting was returned by the publishers with the words, "O.K. But needs stickers down arms and on face. Plain bright tee shirt", scribbled across it. The twins were always mindful of the publisher's requirements.

Janet Johnstone & Anne Grahame Johnstone. The Johnstone twins were experts at painting the detail of period costumes

Paul Gallico's *Miracle in the Wilderness* (1975). These letters reveal how there was considerable pressure to ensure the text and illustrations were ready for a concerted marketing and advertising campaign to coincide with Christmas. The author in one letter makes a few suggestions about what sort of scenes he would like

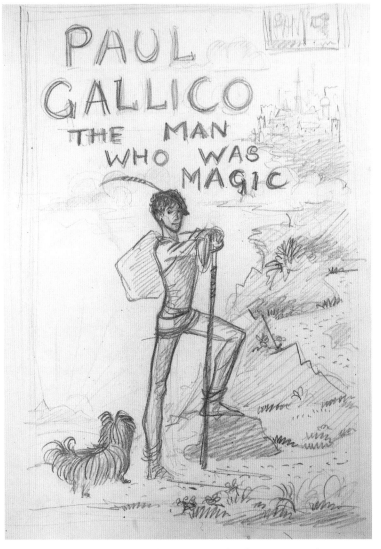

A preliminary design by the Johnstone twins for the dust cover of The Man Who Was Magic *(1968) by Paul Gallico.*

to see illustrated and indicates he has forwarded the Johnstone twins photocopies of engravings illustrating Native American history to aid their research. Paul Gallico writes in another letter to Nigel Viney, a then Deputy Managing Director at the publishing firm Heinemann, of the "artistic integrity" of the Johnstone twins and acknowledges "their experience with the production side of books as well, their knowledge of paper, printing, format, etc." In another letter to the twins Paul Gallico states that, "I imagine the publisher will want to keep the price of the book down". Nigel Viney, from Heinemann Ltd., states in a letter of response to the author that, "Anne is very well versed in the economics of this sort of operation and the vital need to keep to a reasonable price". The detail of the negotiations centred on timing and format and price make these letters of great interest, as they tell us about the concerns of all interested parties surrounding the creation and publishing and costing of this particular children's book, but also tell us how the twins were respected for their knowledge of the publishing sector and ability to work within strict guidelines and accepting of suggestions for the actual illustrations. Indeed, publishers frequently did not want coloured illustrations from the Johnstone twins due to the associated printing costs. Fortunately the twins were expert draftswomen.

The Johnstone twins excelled in drawing and their skills were often in demand to produce children's book illustrations for penny-pinching publishers. Their genius as colourists should not be allowed to shadow their talents in making these drawings. Some of their best work was in pen and ink, including art work for *The Hundred and One Dalmatians* (1956) by Dodie Smith and *Manxmouse* (1968) by Paul Gallico. Such

Janet Johnstone & Anne Grahame Johnstone, "A young Cavalier"

Janet Johnstone & Anne Grahame Johnstone, sketch for "A young Cavalier"

drawings were always cheaper for the publishers to reproduce and the twins enjoyed the challenges of interpreting the key scenes of a story for their audiences using this media for artistic expression. Some of their most visually exciting, elegant, and enjoyable compositions in pen and ink, but also in gouache, are where the illustrations are designed to frame the blocks of text, or else weave and snake in a procession through the printed words. These compositions encourage the reader (or listener) to contemplate the illustrations and possibly might make the lengthier stories less daunting to some young children just learning how to read. Much of the twins' oeuvre was, however, never intended to illustrate books.

Jigsaw with a design by Janet Johnstone & Anne Grahame Johnstone on the theme "The Arrival of The Snow Queen" for Andersen's World, circa 1976. Picture by courtesy of Colchester & Ipswich Museum Service/Mary May.

Commercial Art

The Johnstone twins were always pleased to be approached by businesses or private individuals with requests for their work. In 1976 the twins signed contracts to help design a theme park in Denmark to be named Andersen's World and based on the fairy tales of Hans Christian Andersen. Unfortunately the main financial backer for this scheme withdrew his support and the project foundered. Had the theme park been built the twins' work would have reached a large audience. Though far smaller in scale and ambition, portraits of pets were infrequent, but enjoyable sidelines. Their work outside their mainstay of children's book illustration tends normally to be stylistically similar, but not necessarily so. The requirements of the commission were always considered and they could work in very different styles.

The twins did occasionally work in other branches or genres of the fine arts. Janet produced some extremely competent and charming wildlife paintings. These often represent the female creatures as mothers together with their offspring. Janet captures the motherly tenderness and vulnerability of the young in these pictures. To some viewers Janet's wildlife paintings may lack a sense of the cruelty of nature, but they are entirely in tune with the sentimental feelings often so cleverly portrayed in her work as a children's book illustrator. These wildlife paintings also capture something of the twins' deep-rooted love and veneration of the natural world.

Anne, particularly in the last years of her life, painted some still lives and landscapes. They are surprising to find amongst Anne's oeuvre for Anne's energetic application of oil paint with a paintbrush is very different in these pictures when compared to the painstaking brush strokes of her book illustrations. The fact she chose to work in oils for these late paintings is in itself unexpected, but coupled with the fact that they are totally different from her usual mode of work makes them even more so. Speculation is futile, but I do wonder if Anne had secretly always yearned to be a very different kind of artist. Maybe Anne longed to be a painter of evocative, moody landscapes, rather than an illustrator, but that the demands to earn a living from her art put such ambitions on permanent hold. It was after all as an illustrator that Anne had carved out a name for herself in the fickle and competitive world of art. For this reason most of the commercial artwork produced by Anne and her twin were in a style more readily recognisable as theirs and associated with their children's book illustrations.

Jigsaw with a design by Janet Johnstone
& Anne Grahame Johnstone for
Andersen's World, circa 1976.
Picture by courtesy of Colchester &
Ipswich Museum Service/Mary May.

Left: *Waddingtons 1000 piece jigsaw with a painting by Anne Grahame Johnstone of an organ grinder and dancing children.* Picture by courtesy of Colchester & Ipswich Museum Service/Mary May.

Below: *Waddingtons Super De luxe 1000 piece limited edition double-sided jigsaw puzzle with Christmas scenes by Anne Grahame Johnstone.* Picture by courtesy of Colchester & Ipswich Museum Service/Mary May.

A design by Anne Grahame Johnstone for a wine bottle label. Picture by courtesy of Colchester & Ipswich Museum Service.

Anne Grahame Johnstone,
"Still Life with Flowers", oil on board, 1997.
Picture by courtesy of Colchester &
Ipswich Museum Service/Mary May.

Opposite: *Anne Grahame Johnstone,*
"Ahakista Harbour Scene", oil on board, 1997.
Picture by courtesy of Colchester & Ipswich
Museum Service/Mary May.

Anne did not sell many oil paintings, but both she and Janet were frequently asked to come up with artwork for a wide range of uses. Their paintings were used for jigsaws and decorated tins. They designed wrapping paper and labels for food items, including wine. One of the most significant sources of income for the Johnstone twins was the use of their work as greetings cards and calendars, especially for Royle Publications. Indeed, literally hundreds of their paintings featured on Christmas cards. Towards the end of Anne's life she painted a series of pictures, which collectively were entitled A Country Childhood.

Janet Johnstone & Anne Grahame Johnstone, "Christmas Log" Christmas wrapping paper design. Picture by courtesy of The Great British Card Company.

Janet Johnstone, "Horses" wrapping paper design. Picture by courtesy of The Great British Card Company.

These proved popular as cards and calendars. Two series of four prints, with one picture to represent each of the seasons, were printed from this A Country Childhood series and ten thousand of each set were sold across Britain and the United States of America. Anne's paintings for A Country Childhood are certainly amongst her best and most appealing work, although some of the most important commissions in terms of the size of audience she and Janet received were for the published spin-offs from popular British children's television programmes of the late 1940s and 1950s.

Tin with a design by the Johnstone twins of horses and ponies. Picture by courtesy of Sevenstories.

Janet Johnstone & Anne Grahame Johnstone produced artwork for this
Andy Pandy Annual (1959).

Watch with Mother

Amongst the most significant artwork created by the Johnstone twins was for early British children's television. By today's standards children's television was very limited and in the late 1940s there was only one solitary television channel, the BBC. The number of receivers could be counted in tens of thousands, in contrast to the millions today. The first children's television slot was called *For the Children*, which was an hour-long package of programmes broadcast from the summer of 1946 on Sunday afternoons between 4.00pm and 5.00pm. This was replaced with *Watch with Mother* in 1953. This was a weekday slot transmitted in the late afternoons around 4.00pm for just a quarter of an hour. It was designed with the notional needs of housewives in mind, who could plan baths and bedtimes around the broadcast. The focus of *Watch with Mother* was the pre-school audience, which was fed a diet of inexpensively made string puppet series. It is these programmes Janet and Anne worked on.

The Johnstone twins produced artwork in relation to the puppet series *Charlie the Cat*, *Tai Lu*, *Andy Pandy*, and *Bill and Ben the Flower Pot Men*. The last two of these programmes have now been re-designed and packaged and broadcast to a new audience. When initially broadcast the timing of these children's programmes was anxiously considered and designed to fit into what was deemed by the BBC to be appropriate domestic routines. The Big Brother aspect to the potential control over people's domestic sphere through broadcasting schedules was

Children in the 1950s watching Andy Pandy.

A still from the popular 1950s children's programme Andy Pandy for which the Johnstone twins produced artwork for the published spin-offs.

A still from the popular 1950s children's television programme "Bill and Ben."

understood by the BBC at that time, especially as television was a form of mass media, which could be used for both good and bad. This too was appreciated by the publishers of the spin-off publications associated with the children's broadcasts, for which the Johnstone twins produced artwork.

Janet and Anne produced illustrations for the books based on the characters from the BBC's children's programmes, as in *Tai-Lu's Birthday Party* (1951) and *Bill and Ben and the Potato Man* (1953). They were also commissioned to produce the artwork for *Ross Salmon and the Horse Thieves* (1956) and *Ross Salmon's Horse Race* (1957), based on the BBC's television broadcaster and one-time cowboy Ross Salmon, although not a part of *Watch with Mother*. With some of the books the twins did not work on the paintings and drawings for these publications alone and

were part of a team of artists, as in *Andy Pandy's Annual* (1959), the other illustrators being Sheila Findlay and Matvyn Wright. The latter illustrator and the Johnstone twins are also associated with the weekly cartoon strip of Andy Pandy and Bill and Ben in the comic *Robin*.

The *Robin* comic appeared each week for an intended audience of under sevens. The twins produced illustrations based on the television programme characters Andy Pandy, Tai-Lu, and Bill and Ben the Flower Pot Men for *Robin* on licence from the BBC. Andy Pandy was always in colour on the front page, remembering here that the television programme was in black and white, so creating considerable appeal. The other characters were produced as black and white strips, although in the late 1950s the Flower Pot Men were also included as coloured illustrations.

Throughout the 1950s the Johnstone twins were part of a team of artists producing illustrations for the children's comic "Robin", including for the comic strips Princess Tai-Lu, and Bill and Ben the Flower-pot Men, and Andy Pandy including his friends Loobie Loo and Teddy.

An illustration for Andy Pandy by the Johnstone twins from the 1950s.
Picture by courtesy of Colchester & Ipswich Museum Service/Mary May.

The front cover of "Ross Salmon and the Horse Thieves" (1956) illustrated by the Johnstone twins and based on the BBC's popular television cowboy.

The front cover of "Ross Salmon's Horse Race" (1957) illustrated by the Johnstone twins and based on the BBC's popular television cowboy.

The front cover of "Tai-Lu's Birthday Party" (1951) by the Johnstone twins and based on the popular children's character of radio and television.

Above left: *An extremely rare and damaged survival of a 1950s sketch by the Johnstone twins with one of the Flower Pot Men and the character little Weed.*

Above right: *A rare surviving preliminary sketch by the Johnstone twins for "Bill and Ben and the Potato Man: A Flower Pot Men Story" (1953).*

The Johnstone twins illustrated the published spin-offs from the BBC's children's programmes of Bill and Ben, including "Bill and Ben and the Potato Man: A Flower Pot Men Story" (1953).

The *Robin* comic was first launched in 1953 and had an initial circulation of 450,000. It was brought on to the market following the huge success of its related comics the *Eagle*, launched in 1950 with a circulation of 750,000 copies a week, and that publication's counterpart *Girl*, targeted as the title suggests at girls. The founder of these comics was the Reverend Marcus Morris, who intended to give his publications a real moral purpose.

Marcus Morris had been appalled at the potentially pernicious, sometimes gratuitously violent content of imported American comics on the minds and behaviour of Britain's youths and children. He set out to produce comics, which could edify and promote a Christian world view, whilst simultaneously being filled with fun and adventure appropriate to the relevant targeted age groups of the various comic publications. *Robin* was part of Morris' world view to promote a wholesome society and each week contained a short story on a Christian or biblical theme. This lies at the heart of the comic publications the Johnstone twins produced illustrations for. Whether or not they personally held similar aims and aspirations for their own art is unknown. It is, however, interesting to note that the twins illustrated numerous children's books with a Christian content including children's prayer books and, most significantly, retellings of the Bible stories by Marcus Morris himself, namely *Robin Bible Stories of the Old Testament* (1961) and *Robin Bible Stories of the New Testament* (1961).

The involvement by the Johnstone twins in a comic such as *Robin* and their work on BBC children's television characters are

The Johnstone twins produced elegant illustrations for "Robin Bible Stories of the Old Testament" (1961) and "Robin Bible Stories of the New Testament" (1961) by Marcus Morris, the founder of children's comics including "Robin" and the "Eagle".

amongst their most important work in terms of audience size. It is this work by the twins, which contributes to our understanding today of juvenile popular tastes in the late 1940s and 1950s Britain – and their parents, guardians, or educators. It can be seen to touch upon some of the anxieties of the immediate post-war period and its attitudes on notions of childhood. Moreover, this artwork based on television characters by the twins, together with much of their oeuvre as a whole, today has a considerable retro appeal as art in its own right and amongst those nostalgic for its associated social values of a bygone era.

Moreover, the illustrations of the Johnstone sisters possess an enchanting quality, which appeals to many children's and grown-ups' sense of wonder. The twins often portray a realm where animals have human emotions, teddy bears can be engaging sentient friends, and the world generally is a more delightful and less threatening place, where good triumphs over evil and everything ends happily ever after. Perhaps this all seems too escapist, childish, and unreal, and yet we must remind ourselves here of the charming, yet bizarre fact that: Once upon a time, deep in the Suffolk countryside, there lived identical twin sisters, who on occasion were known to invite their pony to tea.

The Johnstone twins illustrated numerous children's prayer books.

46

Gallery

Janet Johnstone & Anne Grahame Johnstone, "Pussy Cat, Pussy Cat, Where have you been?" Illustration from Dean's Mother Goose Book of Rhymes *(1977).* Picture by courtesy of Andrew Johnstone.

Opposite: *Janet Johnstone & Anne Grahame Johnstone. The big, bad wolf gets his comeuppance.* Picture by courtesy of Andrew Johnstone.

Janet Johnstone & Anne Grahame Johnstone, "Young Boy playing with his Toy Soldiers" from A Child's Garden of Verse *(1971) by R. L. Stevenson.* Picture by courtesy of Andrew Johnstone.

Janet Johnstone & Anne Grahame Johnstone, "Humpty Dumpty". Picture by courtesy of Andrew Johnstone.

Opposite: *Janet Johnstone & Anne Grahame Johnstone, Aladdin commanded by the magician to fetch the lamp from Dean's* Gift Book of Fairy Tales *(1967).* Picture by courtesy of Andrew Johnstone.

Opposite:
*Janet Johnstone &
Anne Grahame
Johnstone,
'D' from an ABC
book of circa 1973.*

*Janet Johnstone &
Anne Grahame
Johnstone,
'E' from an ABC
book of circa 1973.*

*Janet Johnstone &
Anne Grahame
Johnstone, 'Y' from*
A Book of Children's
Rhymes and Verse
(1973).

*Janet Johnstone &
Anne Grahame
Johnstone, 'O' from*
A Book of Children's
Rhymes and Verse
(1973).

*Janet Johnstone & Anne
Grahame Johnstone, 'A' is
for Andrew, circa 1973.*
Picture by courtesy of
Andrew Johnstone.

Anne Grahame Johnstone, a pen and ink drawing for "The Silver Horse" from A Patchwork of Ponies *(1997) by Mary May.*
Picture by courtesy of Colchester & Ipswich Museum Service/Mary May.

Anne Grahame Johnstone, a pen and ink drawing for "The Gale" from A Patchwork of Ponies *(1997) by Mary May.*
Picture by courtesy
of Colchester & Ipswich Museum Service/Mary May.

Anne Grahame Johnstone, a pen and ink drawing for "The Decision" from A Patchwork of Ponies *(1997) by Mary May.* Picture by courtesy of Colchester & Ipswich Museum Service/ Mary May.

Anne Grahame Johnstone, a pen and ink drawing for Piebald is Lucky *(1995) by Mary May.*
Picture by courtesy of Colchester & Ipswich Museum Service/Mary May.

Opposite: *Anne Grahame Johnstone, a pen and ink drawing for* Piebald is Lucky *(1995) by Mary May.*
Picture by courtesy of Colchester & Ipswich Museum Service/Mary May.

Anne Grahame Johnstone, a pen and ink drawing for Deep Water at Dereen *(1996) by Mary May.*
Picture by courtesy of Colchester & Ipswich Museum Service/Mary May.

Anne Grahame Johnstone, a pen and ink drawing for Deep Water at Dereen *(1996) by Mary May.* Picture by courtesy of Colchester & Ipswich Museum Service/Mary May.

Janet Johnstone & Anne Grahame Johnstone, "The Mushroom Ring". Picture by courtesy of Andrew Johnstone.

Janet Johnstone & Anne Grahame Johnstone,
"The Hunter". Picture by courtesy of Andrew Johnstone.

Janet Johnstone & Anne Grahame Johnstone,
"The Woodsman". Picture by courtesy of Andrew Johnstone.

The Johnstone twins loved to paint and draw representations of cats as in this illustration.

Janet Johnstone & Anne Grahame Johnstone,
a scene from Mother Goose.
Picture by courtesy of Andrew Johnstone.

Janet Johnstone & Anne Grahame Johnstone, a scene from "Beauty and the Beast" included in Dean's Gift Book of Fairy Tales *(1967).*
Picture by courtesy of Andrew Johnstone.

Janet Johnstone & Anne Grahame Johnstone, Sir Lancelot kills the Black Knight from Roger Lancelyn Green's Sir Lancelot of the Lake *(1966).* Picture by courtesy of Andrew Johnstone.

Janet Johnstone & Anne Grahame
Johnstone, "Winter Time" from
A Child's Garden of Verse
(1971) by R. L. Stevenson.
Picture by courtesy of
Andrew Johnstone.

Janet Johnstone & Anne Grahame Johnstone, a scene from "Hansel and Gretel" included in Dean's Gift Book of Fairy Tales *(1967).* Picture by courtesy of Andrew Johnstone.

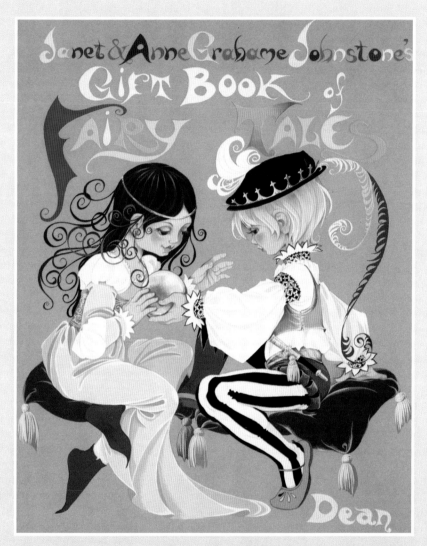

A dust cover design by the Johnstone twins for Dean's Gift Book of Fairy Tales *(1964).* Picture courtesy of Andrew Johnstone.

Janet Johnstone & Anne Grahame Johnstone, illustration of a cowboy praying.
Picture by courtesy of Andrew Johnstone.

Janet Johnstone & Anne Grahame Johnstone, illustration for a card design with a girl and robin in winter. Picture by courtesy of Andrew Johnstone.

*A detailed illustration of a Cavalier
by the Johnstone twins.*

*Janet Johnstone & Anne Grahame
Johnstone, illustration of a Cavalier.*
Picture by courtesy of Andrew Johnstone.

Janet Johnstone & Anne Grahame Johnstone,
illustration of a Cavalier with a monkey.
Picture by courtesy of Andrew Johnstone.

Pen and ink drawing by the Johnstone twins for The Hundred and One Dalmatians *(1956) by Dodie Smith.*
Picture by courtesy of the Howard Gotlieb Archival Research Center, Boston University.

Pen and ink drawing by the Johnstone twins for The Hundred and One Dalmatians *(1956) by Dodie Smith.* Picture by courtesy of the Howard Gotlieb Archival Research Center, Boston University.

Pen and ink drawing by the Johnstone twins for The Hundred and One Dalmatians *(1956) by Dodie Smith.* Picture by courtesy of the Howard Gotlieb Archival Research Center, Boston University.

Pen and ink drawing by the Johnstone twins for The Hundred and One Dalmatians *(1956) by Dodie Smith.*
Picture by courtesy of the Howard Gotlieb Archival Research Center, Boston University.

Pen and ink drawing by the Johnstone twins for The Hundred and One Dalmatians *(1956) by Dodie Smith.*
Picture by courtesy of the Howard Gotlieb Archival Research Center, Boston University.

Pen and ink drawing by the Johnstone twins for The Hundred and One Dalmatians *(1956) by Dodie Smith.* Picture by courtesy of the Howard Gotlieb Archival Research Center, Boston University.

Pen and ink drawing by the Johnstone twins for The Hundred and One Dalmatians *(1956) by Dodie Smith.* Picture by courtesy of the Howard Gotlieb Archival Research Center, Boston University.

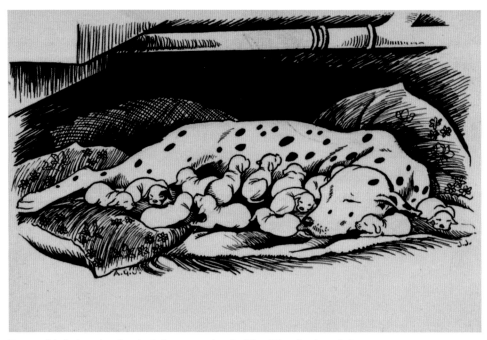

Pen and ink drawing by the Johnstone twins for The Hundred and One
Dalmatians *(1956) by Dodie Smith.*
Picture by courtesy of the Howard Gotlieb Archival Research Center, Boston University.

Pen and ink drawing by the Johnstone twins for The Hundred and One Dalmatians *(1956) by Dodie Smith.*
Picture by courtesy of the Howard Gotlieb Archival Research Center, Boston University.

Pen and ink drawing by the Johnstone twins for The Hundred and One Dalmatians *(1956) by Dodie Smith.*
Picture by courtesy of the Howard Gotlieb Archival Research Center, Boston University.

Pen and ink drawing by the Johnstone twins for The Hundred and One Dalmatians *(1956) by Dodie Smith.*
Picture by courtesy of the Howard Gotlieb Archival Research Center, Boston University.

Pen and ink drawing by the Johnstone twins for The Hundred and One Dalmatians (1956) *by Dodie Smith.*
Picture by courtesy of the Howard Gotlieb Archival Research Center, Boston University.

Below: *Pen and ink drawing by the Johnstone twins for* The Hundred and One Dalmatians (1956) *by Dodie Smith.*
Picture by courtesy of the Howard Gotlieb Archival Research Center, Boston University.

Right: *Pen and ink drawing by the Johnstone twins for* The Hundred and One Dalmatians (1956) *by Dodie Smith.*
Picture by courtesy of the Howard Gotlieb Archival Research Center, Boston University.

Pen and ink drawing by the Johnstone twins for The Hundred and One Dalmatians *(1956) by Dodie Smith.*
Picture by courtesy of the Howard Gotlieb Archival Research Center, Boston University.

A design by Janet Johnstone and Anne Grahame Johnstone for a frontispiece to I Capture the Castle *by Dodie Smith.*

Designs for dust jackets by the Johnstone twins for Blue Bird Picture Books *(1960).*

Opposite: *Janet Johnstone & Anne Grahame Johnstone,*
"Young Soldier on a Rocking Horse:
Portrait of Andrew Johnstone", early 1970s.
Picture by courtesy of Andrew Johnstone.

Anne Grahame Johnstone, a scene for
"Hansel and Gretel", circa 1967.
Picture by courtesy of Andrew Johnstone.

Opposite:
Anne Grahame Johnstone,
"Posting by Pony".
Picture by courtesy of The Great
British Card Company.

Anne Grahame Johnstone,
"Hobby Horse Procession".
Picture by courtesy of
The Great British Card Company.

Janet Johnstone, "Badger and Cubs".
Picture by courtesy of The Great British Card Company.

Janet Johnstone, "Woodmouse".
Picture by courtesy of The Great British Card Company.

Anne Grahame Johnstone, "Frog and Dragonfly".
Picture by courtesy of The Great British Card Company.

Janet Johnstone, "Wild Ponies".
Picture by courtesy of The Great British Card Company.

Janet Johnstone, "Grey Mare and Foal".
Picture by courtesy of The Great British Card Company.

Janet Johnstone, "Vixen and Cubs".
Picture by courtesy of The Great British Card Company.

Opposite: *Janet Johnstone, "Rabbits".*
Picture by courtesy of The Great British Card Company.

Janet Johnstone, "Pheasants".
Picture by courtesy of The Great British Card Company.

Janet Johnstone, "Otter and Cubs".
Picture by courtesy of The Great British Card Company.

Anne Grahame Johnstone,
"Country Childhood".
Picture by courtesy of
The Great British Card Company.

Opposite:
Anne Grahame Johnstone,
"Mothering Sunday".
Picture by courtesy of
The Great British Card Company.

Anne Grahame Johnstone,
"Summer Sewing".
Picture by courtesy of The
Great British Card Company.

Anne Grahame Johnstone,
"Kitten Rescue".
Picture by courtesy of
The Great British Card Company.

Anne Grahame Johnstone,
"Mushrooming".
Picture by courtesy of
The Great British Card Company.

Opposite:
Anne Grahame Johnstone,
"Secret Garden".
Picture by courtesy of
The Great British Card Company.

Anne Grahame Johnstone,
"Hide and Seek".
Picture by courtesy of
The Great British Card Company.

Opposite:
Anne Grahame Johnstone,
"Haymaking".
Picture by courtesy of
The Great British Card Company.

Anne Grahame Johnstone,
"Children in a Meadow".
Picture by courtesy of
The Great British Card Company.

Anne Grahame Johnstone,
"Children and Dog Birdwatching at a Window".
Picture by courtesy of
The Great British Card Company.

Anne Grahame Johnstone,
"Village Wedding".
Picture by courtesy of
The Great British Card Company.

Pen and ink drawing by the Johnstone twins for The Starlight Barking *(1967) by Dodie Smith.*
Picture by courtesy of the Howard Gotlieb Archival Research Center, Boston University.

Pen and ink drawing by the Johnstone twins for The Starlight Barking *(1967) by Dodie Smith.* Picture by courtesy of the Howard Gotlieb Archival Research Center, Boston University.

Pen and ink drawing by the Johnstone twins for
The Starlight Barking *(1967) by Dodie Smith.*
Picture by courtesy of the Howard Gotlieb Archival Research Center,
Boston University.

Pen and ink drawing by the Johnstone twins for
The Starlight Barking *(1967) by Dodie Smith.*
Picture by courtesy of the Howard Gotlieb Archival Research Center,
Boston University.

Pen and ink drawing by the Johnstone twins for The Starlight Barking *(1967) by Dodie Smith.* Picture by courtesy of the Howard Gotlieb Archival Research Center, Boston University.

Pen and ink drawing by the Johnstone twins for The Starlight Barking *(1967) by Dodie Smith.*
Picture by courtesy of the Howard Gotlieb Archival Research Center, Boston University.

Pen and ink drawing by the Johnstone twins for The Starlight Barking *(1967) by Dodie Smith.* Picture by courtesy of the Howard Gotlieb Archival Research Center, Boston University.

Pen and ink drawing by the Johnstone twins for The Starlight Barking *(1967) by Dodie Smith.*
Picture by courtesy of the Howard Gotlieb Archival Research Center, Boston University.

Anne Grahame Johnstone, "Oranges and Lemons".
Picture by courtesy of The Great British Card Company.

A design by the Johnstone twins for a dust jacket, circa 1972.

A design by the Johnstone twins for a dust cover, circa 1972.

Anne Grahame Johnstone, "Gathering Berries".
Picture by courtesy of The Great British Card Company.

Opposite: *Anne Grahame Johnstone, "Teddy Bears' Picnic".*
Picture by courtesy of The Great British Card Company.

Anne Grahame Johnstone, "The Swallows".
Picture by courtesy of The Great British Card Company.

Anne Grahame Johnstone, "Nativity Set".
Picture by courtesy of The Great British Card Company.

Anne Grahame Johnstone, "Ploughboys' Chorus".
Picture by courtesy of The Great British Card Company.

Anne Grahame Johnstone, "Return from the Pub".
Picture by courtesy of The Great British Card Company.

Anne Grahame Johnstone, "Snow King".
Picture by courtesy of
The Great British Card Company.

Opposite:
Anne Grahame Johnstone,
"Children Posting Christmas Cards".
Picture by courtesy of The Great
British Card Company.

Anne Grahame Johnstone, "Three Kings".
Picture by courtesy of The Great British Card Company.

Opposite: *Anne Grahame Johnstone,*
"The End of the Day".
Picture by courtesy of The Great British Card Company.

Anne Grahame Johnstone,
"Can You Hear Anything?"
Picture by courtesy of The
Great British Card Company.

Janet Johnstone & Anne Grahame Johnstone, "St Nicholas" Christmas card. Picture by courtesy of The Great British Card Company.

Anne Grahame Johnstone, illustration of a Christmas scene.
Picture by courtesy of Andrew Johnstone.

Opposite:
Anne Grahame Johnstone,
"Toy Shop".
Picture by courtesy of
The Great British Card Company.

Suggestions for Further Reading

Below is a short list of works covering themes related to this monograph and is intended as a guide, rather than an exhaustive bibliography. For a list of books containing illustrations by the Johnstone twins please refer to the appendix.

- Chapman, James, *British Comics: A Cultural History*, London, 2011.
- Grove, Valerie, *Dear Dodie: The Life of Dodie Smith*, London, 1996.
- Kelleway, Philip, *Highly Desirable: The Zinkeisen Sisters and Their Legacy*, Leiston, 2008.
- Morris, Sally & Jan Hallwood, *Living with Eagles: Priest to Publisher: The Life and Times of Marcus Morris*, Cambridge, 1998.
- Oswell, David, "Watching with Mother in the early 1950s", in: Cary Bazalgette & David Buckingham (ed.s), *In Front of the Children: Screen Entertainment and Young Audiences*, London, 1997 [First pub. 1995], pp.34-46.
- Reid, Betty & Anthony, "Janet and Anne Grahame Johnstone: Illustrators of over 200 children's books", in: *Book and Magazine Collector*, No.204, March 2001, pp.48-63.
- Whalley, Joyce Irene & Tessa Rose Chester, *A History of Children's Book Illustration*, London, 1988.

Appendix

This appendix contains a chronological list of children's books and other titles illustrated and/or written by Janet Johnstone and Anne Grahame Johnstone. As re-printed and foreign language editions have been excluded, this bibliographic list should be treated strictly as a guide only.

Janet & Anne Grahame Johnstone, *Touchstone*, New York (Reinhart & Co.), 1947.

Jonathan Swift, *Gulliver's Travels*, London (Treasure Library), undated, circa 1950.

Heinrich Hoffmann, *Struwwelpeter, or Merry Stories and Funny Pictures*, London (John Gifford), 1950.

Johanna Spyri, *Heidi*, London (Heirloom Library), undated, 1950s assumed.

Janet & Anne Grahame Johnstone, *Your Pantomime Book*, London (Heirloom Library), undated, 1950s assumed.

Charles Kingsley, *The Water Babies*, London (Heirloom Library), undated, 1950s assumed.

Shelagh Fraser & Billy Thatcher, *Tai-Lu's Birthday Party: Twirly Book No.5*, London (Publicity Products Limited), 1951.

Shelagh Fraser & Billy Thatcher, *Tai-Lu Talking*, London (Heinemann), 1952.

Maria Bird, *Bill & Ben & the Potato Man*, London (Publicity Products Limited), 1953.

Lorna Hill, *Dancing Peel*, London (Nelson), 1954.

Ida Foulis, *This Land of Kings*, London (Ward, Lock & Co.), 1954 and 1957.

Ada Orchard (ed. Jean Sutcliffe), *Charlie the Cat: Listen with Mother Tales*, London (Adprint), 1954.

Lorna Hill, *Dancer's Luck*, London (Nelson), 1955.

Lorna Hill, *The Little Dancer*, London (Nelson), 1956.

Ross Salmon, *Ross Salmon & the Horse Thieves*, London (Adprint), 1956.

Dodie Smith, *The Hundred & One Dalmatians*, London (Heinemann), 1956.

Frances Sybil Victoria Sutton Vane, *The Black Whippet*, New York (Viking Press), 1957.

Ross Salmon, *Ross Salmon's Horse Race*, London (Adprint), 1957.

Antonia White, *Minka & Curdy*, Harvill, 1957.

Lorna Hill, *Dancer in the Wings*, London (Nelson), 1958.

John Pudney, *Crossing the Road*, London (Hamish Hamilton), 1958.

Andy Pandy's Annual, London (Purnell), 1959.

Jacob Ludwig Carl Grimm & Wilhelm Carl Grimm (translated by Ruth Michaelis-Jena & Arthur Ratcliff), *New Tales from Grimm*, Edinburgh & London (W. & R. Chambers), 1960.

Vivian Ellis, *Hilary's Tune*, London (Max Parrish), 1960.

Diana Marr Johnson, *Eight Rainbow Tales*, London (Dean & Son), 1960.

Vivian Ellis, *Hilary's Holidays*, London (Max Parrish), 1961.

The Blue Bird Picture Books, Edinburgh & London (W. & R. Chambers), 1960/1961.

Marcus Morris, *Robin Bible Stories of the Old Testament*, London (Longacre Press), 1961.

Marcus Morris, *Robin Bible Stories of the New Testament*, London (Longacre Press), 1961.

The Arabian Nights, London (Ward, Lock & Co.), 1963.

Roger Lancelyn Green, *Tales of the Greeks & Trojans*, London (Purnell), 1964.

Janet & Anne Grahame Johnstone, *Dean's Gold Medal Book of Fairy Tales: Cinderella; Babes in the Wood; Sleeping Beauty; Puss in Boots*, London (Dean & Son), 1964.

Jean Bashfield (retelling of William Schwenck Gilbert's & Arthur Sullivan's opera), *The Pirates of Penzance*, London (Nelson & Sons), 1965.

Dean's Gift Book of Nursery Rhymes, London (Dean & Son), 1965.

Nursery Rhymes Old & New, London (Dean & Son), circa 1965.

Gold Star Book of Ride-A-Cock Horse Nursery Rhymes, London (Dean & Son), circa 1965.

Roger Lancelyn Green, *Myths from Many Lands*, London (Purnell), 1965.

Enid Blyton (retells), *Tales of Long Ago*, London (Dean & Son), 1965.

Roger Lancelyn Green, *Folk Tales of the World*, London (Purnell), 1966.

Roger Lancelyn Green, *Sir Lancelot of the Lake*, London (Purnell), 1966.

Martha Mearns (retelling of William Schwenck Gilbert's & Arthur Sullivan's opera), *The Yeomen of the Guard*, Edinburgh & London (Nelson), 1966.

Jean Blashfield, *Iolanthe*, London (Nelson), 1966.

Anne Grahame Johnstone (with illustrations by Janet), *ABC of Nature*, London (Dean), 1966.

Jean Blashfield, *The Gondoliers*, London (Nelson), 1966.

Martha Mearns (retelling of William Schwenck Gilbert's & Arthur Sullivan's opera), *HMS Pinafore*, London (Nelson), 1966.

Dodie Smith, *The Starlight Barking*, London (Heinemann), 1967.

Dean's *Gift Book of Fairy Tales*, London (Dean & Son), 1967.

Paul Gallico, *Manxmouse*, London (Heinemann), 1968.

Greek Myths & Legends, London (MacDonald Educational), 1968.

Roger Lancelyn Green, *Jason & the Golden Fleece*, London (Purnell), 1968.

Lewis Carroll, *Alice in Wonderland*, World Distributors, 1968.

Paul Gallico, *The Man Who Was Magic*, London (Pan Books), 1968.

Janet Grahame Johnstone (with illustrations by Janet & Anne Grahame Johnstone), *A Child's Book of Prayers*, London (Dean), 1968.

Little One's Prayers, London (Dean), 1968.

Honoria Plesch & Mafia Stevens, *Rainbow the Cook Pop-up Book*, London (Dean), 1969.

John Morais Montgomery (selected by), *The Best Cat Stories*, London (Pan Books), 1969.

Honoria Plesch & Mafia Stevens, *Seven Rainbow Tales*, London (Dean), 1969.

Robert Browning, *The Pied Piper of Hamelin*, London (Dean & Son), 1969.

Anne Grahame Johnstone (with illustrations by Janet), *My Picture Book of Animals*, London (Dean), 1970.

Gianni Rodari (translated by Patrick Creagh), *La Freccia Azzurra: The Benfana's Toyshop*, a Twelfth Night Story, London (Dent), 1970.

Dodie Smith, *A Tale of Two Families*, London (Heinemann), 1970.

Janet Johnstone (with illustrations by Janet & Anne Grahame Johnstone), *Puppy Dog Nursery Rhymes*, London (Dean), 1970.

Janet Johnstone (with illustrations by Janet & Anne Grahame Johnstone), *Pussy Cat Nursery Rhymes*, London (Dean), 1970.

A Book of Fairy Tales, London (Dean), 1970.

Eileen Esther Passmore, *My Baby Jesus Pop-up Book*, London (Dean), 1970.

Norah Lofts, *The Study of Maude Reed*, London (Transworld Publishers), 1971.

Another Book of Fairy Tales: Rumpelstiltskin; Jack & the Beanstalk; The Frog Prince; The Princess & the Pea, London (Dean), 1971.

Nursery Rhyme Treasury, Young World Productions, 1971.

R. L. Stevenson, *A Child's Garden of Verse*, London (Dean), 1971.

Madame La Comtesse D'Aulnoy, *The White Cat*, London (Dean), 1972.

Norah Lofts, *Rupert Hatton's Tale*, Carousel Books, 1972.

An Enchanting Book of Nursery Rhymes, London (Dean), 1972.

Janet & Anne Grahame Johnstone's Gift Book of Fairy Tales, London (Dean), 1973.

Janet Johnstone (with illustrations by Janet & Anne Grahame Johnstone), *A, Apple Pie, B, Bit It*, London (Dean), 1973.

Sallie Walrond, *Encyclopaedia of Driving*, Ilkley (Scolar Press), 1974.

Alan Blackwood (compiled by), *Mulberry Bush Book of Nursery Rhymes*, London (Nelson Young World), 1974.

Janet Johnstone (with illustrations by Janet & Anne Grahame Johnstone), *More Prayers for Children*, London (Dean), 1974.

Dean's Gift Book of Bible Stories, London (Dean), 1974.

Dean's Book of Famous Fairy Tales, Stories after Hans Christian Andersen, London (Dean), 1974.

Gift Book of Hans Christian Andersen Fairy Tales, London (Dean), 1975.

Mae Broadley (selected & rewritten by), *Tales from Everywhere*, Manchester (World Distributors), 1975.

Paul Gallico, *Miracle in the Wilderness*, London (Heinemann),

1975.

Dean's Gold Medal Book of Rhymes, London (Dean), 1975.

Janet & Anne Grahame Johnstone's Gift Book of Prayers for Children, London (Dean), 1975.

New Little Prayers Pop-up Book, London (Dean), 1976.

Janet Johnstone (with illustrations by Janet & Anne Grahame Johnstone), *Little Jesus Pop-up Book*, London (Dean), 1976.

Janet & Anne Grahame Johnstone, *Dean's Gold Star Book of Cowboys*, London (Dean), 1976.

Supreme Book of Children's Prayers, London (Dean), 1977.

Virginia Salmon (retold by), *Dean's Supreme Book of Bible Stories*, London (Dean), 1977.

Dean's Mother Goose Book of Rhymes, Playmore Inc. Publishers, 1977.

Janet & Anne Grahame Johnstone, *Dean's Gold Star Book of Indians*, London (Dean), 1977.

Dean's Gift Book of Nursery Rhymes Old & New, London (Dean), 1978. A number of the rhymes and illustrations in this edition were previously published in *Nursery Rhymes Old & New* and *Gold Star Book of Ride-a-Cock-Horse Nursery Rhymes*.

Bible Stories & Prayers for Children, London (Dean), 1978. Text and illustrations in this edition were previously published in *Dean's Gift Book of Bible Stories* and *Gift Book of Prayers for Children*.

Janet & Anne Grahame Johnstone, *A Book of Children's Rhymes*, London (Dean), 1978.

Dodie Smith, *The Midnight Kittens*, London (W. H. Allen), 1978.

Fiberarts: The Magazine of Textiles, September – October, USA, 1978.

Fiberarts: The Magazine of Textiles, November – December, USA, 1978.

Fiberarts: The Magazine of Textiles, January – February, USA, 1979.

Fiberarts: The Magazine of Textiles, May – June, USA, 1979.

Fiberarts: The Magazine of Textiles, September – October, USA, 1979.

Janet & Anne Grahame Johnstone, *Ten Little Dogs*, Cambridge (Brimax Books), 1979.

Enid Blyton, *The Enchanted Wood*, London (Dean), 1979.

Janet & Anne Grahame Johnstone, *Cowboys & Indians*, London (Dean), 1979. Previously published as *Dean's Gold Star Book of Indians* and *Dean's Gold Star Book of Cowboys*.

Little Tot's Book of Nursery Rhymes, London (Dean), 1979. Note that the illustrators are unnamed in this edition.

The Wonderful Story of Sleeping Beauty, London (Dean), 1979.

The Wonderful Story of Puss in Boots, London (Dean), 1979.

The Wonderful Story of Snow White & the Seven Dwarfs, London (Dean), 1979.

The Wonderful Story of Cinderella, London (Dean), 1979.

Santa Claus is Coming to Town, London (Dean), circa 1979. Illustrations by Anne Grahame Johnstone.

Santa's Toy Shop, London (Dean), circa 1979. Illustrations by Anne Grahame Johnstone.

The Night Before Christmas, London (Dean), 1980. Illustrators unnamed.

Little One's Book of Nursery Rhymes, London (Dean), 1981. No author or illustrator named.

Anne Grahame Johnstone, *My Pop-up Book of Baby Animals*, London (Dean), 1982.

Sallie Walrond, *Your Problem Horse*, London (Pelham Books), 1982.

My Pop-up Book ABC, London (Dean), 1982.

My Pop-up Book of Fairy Tales, London (Dean), 1982.

My Pop-up Book of Nursery Rhymes, London (Dean), 1982.

My Pop-up Book of Cinderella, London, (Deans International), 1983.

My Pop-up Book of Puss in Boots, London (Deans International), 1983.

My Pop-up Book of Snow White & the Seven Dwarfs, London (Deans International), 1983.

My Pop-up Book of Sleeping Beauty, London (Deans International), 1983.

My First Book of Nursery Rhymes, London (Award Publications), 1985.

A Year of Poems, Twickenham (Dean), 1986. Illustrated by Anne Grahame Johnstone.

Jane Carruth (retelling of Charles Kingsley's classic), *The Water Babies*, London (Award Publications), circa 1988. Illustrated by Anne Grahame Johnstone.

Jane Carruth (retelling of James Barrie's classic), *Peter Pan & Wendy*, London (Award Publications), 1988. Illustrated by Anne Grahame Johnstone.

My Book of Enchanting Nursery Rhymes, Treasure, 1989.

My Book of Enchanting Fairy Tales, Treasure, 1989.

Bible Stories & Prayers for Children, Treasure, 1989.

Linda Jennings, *My Christmas Book of Stories and Carols*, London (Award), 1990. Illustrated by Anne Grahame Johnstone.

Mary May, *Piebald is Lucky*, Collingbourne Kingston (Manor Acre), 1995. Illustrated by Anne Grahame Johnstone.

Mary May, *The Will to Win*, Collingbourne Kingston (Manor Acre), 1996. Illustrated by Anne Grahame Johnstone.

Mary May, *Deep Water at Dereen*, Collingbourne Kingston (Manor Acre), 1996. Illustrated by Anne Grahame Johnstone.

Mary May, *A Patchwork of Ponies*, Collingbourne Kingston (Manor Acre), 1997. Illustrated by Anne Garahame Johnstone.

A Year of Poetry, London (Award), 1997. Illustrated by Anne Grahame Johnstone.

Index